# THE JEWEL IN THE SEA

## Based on the True Story of New Zealand

By  Ian Sharplin

The Jewel in the Sea
Based on the true story of New Zealand

ISBN    978-0-473-44016-9 (pbk)
        978-0-473-44017-6 (ePub)
        978-0-473-44018-3 (Kindle)



Cover image adapted by Johno Dempsey
behance.net/manufactorium
from an image by sbarabu/shutterstock.com

Sailing ship image p.3 used with permission from kkokosz.deviantart.com

First published by Read Publishing NZ in 2014
readpublishing.nz

Re-published and distributed by Wild Side Publishing in 2018
wildsidepublishing.com
Northland, New Zealand

International listing Ingram Spark 2018

# Dedication

I dedicate this book to the King above all kings.
Not one whose throne is here on earth,
but the one to whom we sing
the National Anthem of our land;
the one who hears our prayer,
'cause  without the grace of God dear friends,
none of us would be here!

# Contents


Preface ....................................................................................1

**Part One:** ..........................................................................3

1.   Tuki and Huru .............................................................5

2.   Te Pahi's Stand .........................................................11

3.   Samuel Marsden .......................................................17

4.   Ruatara ......................................................................21

5.   Ruatara's Biscuits ....................................................31

6.   Samuel's Sailing Ship ..............................................35

7.   The Ark's Voyage .....................................................39

8.   The Zoo Arrives ........................................................41

9.   NZ's First Christmas – 25 December 1814 ............45

**Part Two:** ........................................................................49

10.  Te Waharoa – Slave Boy to Mighty Chief .............51

11.  Tarore and Ngakuku .................................................61

12.  The Message of the God Book .................................67

13.  The Big Move .............................................................73

14.  The Raiding Party ......................................................81

15.  Utu Stops Here ...........................................................87

16.  The Slave: Ripahau ...................................................91

17.  The Miracle of Forgiveness .....................................95

18.  The Fire Spreads ......................................................105

**Part Three:** ....................................................................107

19.  The Journey South ..................................................109

20.  Katu and Te Whiwhi ................................................111

21.  The Hide Out! ..........................................................117

22.  Return to the Mainland ..........................................125

23.  The Power of Love ...................................................129

24.  Forgiveness Bridges the Gap ................................133

25.  The King Maker ........................................................139

26.  The Jewel in the Sea ...............................................143

**Maori Glossary** ............................................................151

# Preface

The story of New Zealand
should be wrote for all to read.
It seems that if it don't get told
some people won't get freed.

If you've left your war-torn country
for this 'Jewel in the Sea',
I want to give a 'heads-up'
as to why New Zealand's free.

Providence is God's playground
in which we get to play.
History is His Story
in the things we do each day.

Miracles He sends along
to help us all to see,
that nothing's here by accident,
especially you and me.

Man can be blind.
Like little kids we have our way to do it,
but when we're stuck we call to Dad
to help us to get through it.

Our history's full of miracles
to get us out of ruts.
Historians start them with the words,
"Nobody knows why but... "

Often reading of our land
these words begin a story.
"Nobody knows why but... "
Then wham! Adventure! Romance! Glory!

All of life's about people.
Our history proves that's true.
The warmth of hearts, the love of men,
and great adventure too.

There is poetic licence here
but with the events of history too.
I hope this warms up, reaches,
touches, blesses and changes YOU!

# PART 1:
# The Connections

## Chapter 1:

# Tuki and Huru

One day a young man in the North,
he saw a sailing ship.
Tuki grabbed his mate, Huru
and paddled after it.

They stuffed their waka with some things
so they could do a trade,
but what they were about to see
would change their world that day.

The captain of that ship ('Daedalus')
had orders from the British king,
and he would get a hundred pounds
if he could do one thing.

If he could get two Maori men
to sail to Norfolk Isle,
to turn flax bushes into silk
then he would make a pile.

A hundred pounds was heaps back then
in 1792,
so as he watched these warriors come,
he figured what to do.

"Prepare a feast below," he said,
"You men know what to do."
Tuki and Huru climbed on board
and didn't have a clue.

Only those two got on board,
the others all were scared.
These two brave men were shown below
the feast that was prepared.

Captivated by the kai
they'd never seen before,
they ate and ate... and kidnapped,
they sailed off to foreign shores.

The warriors although kidnapped
were allowed to roam the ship.
How come they were not put in chains
or tied a little bit?

"Hey, Huru! We are not tied up!
What is this all about?"
They seemed free. How could that be?
They couldn't make it out.

Norfolk Island was a British
prison at that time.
These boys were not tied up though
'cause they hadn't done a crime!

In fact the captain didn't break our laws
when he kidnapped the men
because New Zealand simply had no laws
to break away back then!

You might think that without rules
New Zealand would be fun!
But nah! You could be kidnapped, speared,
or shot by anyone!

When they reached the island,
longboats surfed in on the waves.
The two friends hopped out on the shore
but didn't feel like slaves.

"Hey, Tuki, when we paddle wakas
we face the way we go,
but did you see the funny way
these Pakeha fellas row?

They don't look where they're going.
Nah!  They face backwards instead.
It might be something that they ate
affects them in the head.

Maybe we could show them
it's best to face the front,
and  have more fellas paddling
so you can get more grunt!

Never mind, we all can learn.
They sure know how to eat,
and the thing they call the 'sailing ship'
is pretty hard to beat!

They make great clothes to keep them warm
when nights are freezing cold.
I think we should team up with them
before we get too old!"

They walked around without a guard
to put them in a cell.
The strangest thing was they were free
as far as they could tell.

In fact the governor, Mr King,
asked them to stay with him.
They had a room in the governor's house,
a mansion just for them!

All they had to do was show
some prisoners how to weave,
but they said, "Nah! That's women's work,
and we just want to leave!"

Now Governor King was kind to them,
he treated them like sons
and his kindness brought its own reward:
in six months they succumbed.

The cloth the prisoners made from flax
was used for fine ships' sails,
enabling ships to sail and trade
and go chasing after whales.

Maori made the finest cloth
the world had seen from flax,
and Tuki and Huru showed them how.
That's just the simple facts.

That year back here in Kiwi land
we all thought they were gone!
When Gov'nor King sailed back with them
we realized we'd been wrong.

"How come the governor let you live?
We all thought you were dead!
But the Pakeha filled his ship with food
to feed us all instead."

Food types they were very scarce
like puha, pork, and fish.
McDonalds? Nah! Wendys? Nah!
Come on, get a grip!

So when King brought potatoes,
all we had was mostly fish.
Imagine when that ship came in...
Hello! Fish & chips!

Now 'Kingi' is a name we use
all over the Far North.
Amazing just what kindness does;
it brings its own rewards.

That was the start of something big.
It's called 'goodwill to men.'
The story of our land moves on
but it started way back then.

## Chapter 2

# Te Pahi's Stand

Te Pahi was a famous chief.
He had five strapping sons.
A mighty man his people loved.
Yep, he was number one!

Tuki and Huru came from there,
from that part of the land,
and this next part of our story
is about Te Pahi's stand.

Now here's the thing, our Mr King
was moved to New South Wales.
A Governor of Australia now,
not Norfolk Island's jails.

In search of Governor King,
Te Pahi sailed to Aussies' shore.
He took his sons to find the man
his people now adored.

On the wharf in Sydney Cove
the Aussies stood amazed.
Six mighty men, honed, pumped and tall.
Whew! Women's eyes were glazed!

The news rang out throughout the land
on that historic day:
the great Te Pahi with his sons
was on Australian clay.

Governor King heard they were there
and invited them to stay
and Te Pahi heard at tea one night
of a trial in the court next day.

He decided to take his sons to court
to learn of the Pakeha laws.
Two men were in the dock that day.
They stole pork from the stores.

"This man is guilty." said the judge,
"I sentence him to die!"
Te Pahi, stunned, he went straight home
and said, "Governor, tell me why?

In my world all men need to eat
and can take food anytime.
Don't steal a man's wife or take his things,
but food is not a crime....

These men can't die for just taking food.
What justice is that for a man?
Just give them a hiding, if you must,
not death.  I must take a stand!"

"Those men must hang," the governor said.
"Our laws they serve us well."
Te Pahi began to weep for the men
and visit them in their cell.

The cell door slammed shut
        and the chief was in shock.
He asked the men, "What can I do?
I will ask for a pardon from Governor King
so you write it all down... what is true!"

So the men wrote for pardon
        to the governor himself
and Te Pahi delivered the plea.
The Governor, though moved
        by the heart of the chief said,
"They surely must die, but I'll see."

Te Pahi got down on his face on the floor
and he pled for the lives of those men.
He wept right out loud as his heart cried out
for one stroke of the governor's pen.

The governor was holding a feast at his house
and inviting some dignitaries
and captains of ships
        that were anchored in port,
all to dine with his guest, Te Pahi!

As all took their fill of the food and the wine,
Te Pahi felt sorrow inside.
He asked, "Governor King,
    will you pardon those men?
Tell me, sir, what it is you decide."

"Those men, they must hang. That is the law.
The stealing of food is a sin."
Te Pahi went quiet, and then turned his head
to the captain sat opposite him.

"If you hang up those men
    you must hang this man up!
This captain he sailed to my shores.
He filled up his ship with potatoes of mine
without asking. He just took them all."

The story was true and the captain went white
as he thought no one saw him that day
when he plundered potatoes
    in the dark of the night
from the chief's crop and just sailed away.

"Is this true," asked the governor,
    "what Te Pahi says?"
And the captain admitted it was.
"So you see," said Te Pahi,
    "all three men must hang
by your laws in this great land of Oz!"

With this news come to light the governor sighed,
and Te Pahi he stood to his feet.
"Until you have pardoned those men in their cells,
Governor King, I simply won't eat!"

For days, in his room, Te Pahi he wept
and he ate not one thing, as he'd said.
The governor, not wanting Te Pahi to die,
pardoned all three men instead!

## Chapter 3

# Samuel Marsden

Not often does a governor
of a nation pardon men.
Te Pahi became famous
for his sense of justice then.

A judge called Samuel Marsden
was amazed by our chief's heart
and in the future of New Zealand
this would play a vital part

Marsden was a magistrate,
his story leads us on.
Samuel was his Christian name,
and Samuel was a Pom!

Sam grew up in England
but King George had work for him.
He sent him to Australia
where convicts' lives were grim.

He sent him as a chaplain
for the hearts of broken men
but it was as a magistrate
his heart was stirred back then.

Inspired by New Zealand's Chief
Te Pahi's love for men,
he opened up his diary and
he reached out for his pen.

He wrote, "I believe Maori to be
a quite superior race
and if the Gospel of Jesus Christ
is taken to that place,
New Zealand will become one of
the finest lands on earth!"
And deep inside he wished
that he may live to see that birthed!

Adventure flowed through Samuel's veins
and kindness was his way.
He put aside some land he owned
that he would give away.

He realized that the Maori boys
who worked on whaling ships
were stationed sometimes in that port
so he made the best of it.

All Maori men were welcomed
on the farm that was his own.
He fed them, taught them how to ride
and they could call it home.

They'd never seen a horse
until they stepped onto that land
but Sam was like a dad to them.
They learned heaps from this man.

Many boys stayed on the farm.
It was like adventure land.
When there were chores and stuff to do
the boys would give a hand.

One boy called Ruatara,
Samuel got to know real well
and it was good that they had met
as later times would tell.

He was amazed by these young men,
their strength and will to learn,
and with them his own passion grew
for the land of the silver fern.

Sam knew that there were many things
they didn't have at home—
horses, sheep and cows to milk
and crops that could be grown.

He prayed to God that one day soon
he'd make it to our shore
to see these ones he'd grown to love
and give them so much more!

Chapter 4:

# Ruatara

Ruatara, the warrior prince,
his father was a chief
and Te Pahi was his uncle
way before this land had beef.

In fact we hardly had a thing.
No shopping in the land.
You had to paddle, walk, or run,
and work was done by hand.

So girls were fit and men were honed
and everyone looked great,
but Ruatara's dream to see the world
just couldn't wait.

His uncle had gone overseas
and soon his time would come.
He got aboard a whaling ship
and he expected fun.

His one desire: to meet King George,
His Majesty the King—
but once on board the *Argo*
well now, that changed everything.

They treated Maori boys like stink
on board some whaling ships,
and many times for no good cause
the captain used the whips.

One captain's name was Moody.
Santa Anna was his ship.
Bounty was an island in the south
with seals on it!

(Moody had a bright idea
to fill his money tins.
In London he could trade for cash
if he could find seal skins.)

Ruatara and some friends
were put there at high tide.
Left to survive on Bounty Isle,
and three of those men died.

For weeks they were just left there
with no food and no supplies.
It was bitter, bleak and freezing.
No wonder those men died.

Eight thousand seal skins were amassed
before the ship returned.
Amazing, his survival skills,
amazing what he'd learned.

But persevere this fine prince did
until he nearly died.
Worn out and sick, but at last the ship
to London's dock was tied.

So close and yet so far away
he begged the captain's leave
to meet King George, that was his dream,
but the story had a weave.

The captain didn't want to have
a dead boy on his ship
so had him transferred to a boat
with criminals on it.

That boat sailed for southern seas,
Australia was its fate.
Now underneath an old greatcoat
Ruatara had to wait.

He couldn't move, he was so sick,
but sometimes he would cough
and hope if someone noticed him
they'd help him to get off.

They sailed to Portsmouth on the way
to take on board a man.
That man was Samuel Marsden
and the miracles began.

Samuel saw the greatcoat cough—
a strange sight to be sure.
He lifted up the coat to see
the boy he'd known before.

Ruatara had no tattoos
on his face or on his arm,
so Samuel knew him straight away
from staying on the farm.

What are the odds? How high you think?
There is a God above!
There was no white man on the earth
would show this boy more love.

Samuel Marsden's mentor was
William Wilberforce.
He abolished slavery,
but not alone of course.

A mutual friend of both these men,
John Newton was his name,
he wrote 'Amazing Grace'
and you'll know that song by name.

John had captained many ships
on which the slaves had died.
Then one day he encountered God
from whom he couldn't hide.

Meeting God like that
caused the man to change his ways.
He now helped William Wilberforce
to set free all the slaves.

To check what someone's like inside
look at the friends they choose.
These men were Samuel Marsden's friends,
Ruatara couldn't lose.

Samuel had him seen to
by the surgeon on the ship.
He got the best of treatment.
Samuel made quite sure of it.

The lad was saved from certain death
while sailing with his friend,
and both learned one another's tongue
before that journey's end.

"Why do you fight, why do you war
when you don't have a foe?
Who is the enemy of your land?
I'd really like to know."

Ruatara said, "We've always fought.
It's just the thing we do.
I think it's pride makes men take sides.
Let me explain to you....

When someone does something to you
my people get them back.
They tell the chief, he tells the tribe,
together they attack....

So there it is, if they hurt you,
we hurt them back again.
We call that 'utu' in our land
and you call it 'revenge.'"

But heaps of times when Maori boys
were staying on the farm,
they had such fun together
and none had come to harm.

They came from different tribes and yet
enjoyed each other well.
Then Samuel had a bright idea.
Yep. Ding dong, rang the bell!

"When you return, go see the chiefs
and you invite their sons.
I'll pay their passage over here
away from dads and mums.

Together they can just have fun
and they'll become great friends
and one day they will be the chiefs.
Then the fighting ends!

Your mother has five brothers, right?
And they're all famous men.
Hongi, Moka, and the rest,
just start by asking them."

It was true, he knew most chiefs
from being who he was,
so he would set out asking
if their sons could visit Oz!

Until he got his strength back
he stayed on Samuel's farm.
Samuel gave him land, his own,
which kept him out of harm.

He learned how wheat plucked from the tops
of stalks could give you bread
unlike potatoes where they grow
beneath the ground instead.

Samuel made a note
that Ruatara never swore
and nor did his companions
which impressed him even more!

"The more I see these people,"
Samuel wrote for all to read,
"the more I am impressed
by their morals and their creed."

No one knows why but these two,
the Maori and the Pom,
had so much influence on men
for good that still goes on.

Ruatara held some values
that men do well to keep.
His tribe was influenced by them
so let's just take a peep....

When the good ship *Active* dropped supplies
in the bay close by his shore:
tea, sugar, clothing, flour, seeds
and often so much more,

they'd leave it all unlocked
in a storehouse on the beach.
Those things were just like gold dust
yet in everybody's reach.

Ruatara, lived inland
26 kilometres more,
and they just left this gold dust out there
miles from his front door.

But no one touched it
though it could be pinched at anytime,
'cause Maori considered theft to be
a really wicked crime.

'Tiketike no e Teka!'
(A chieftain never lies)
was a saying men could bank on
and that saved many lives.

"The hearts of these great warriors
are finer than our own!"
was something Pakeha leaders
were often heard to moan.

You could trust a chieftain's word
upon your very life.
If leaders were like that nowadays
wouldn't that be nice?

There was no Maori word for 'horse'—
our people hadn't seen one—
and Ruatara had a job
convincing us there'd been one.

"A big black 'kuri'!" he would say.
That means a big black dog!
Suppose at least that looks more like
a horse than, say, a frog.

If you're the first to see something
that no one's ever seen,
then you could tell the people
 that the colour blue is green.

They don't have a clue unless
you draw it out by hand.
Sometimes he would draw stuff
with a stick down on the sand.

'Horse and carriage', there's a sight,
but it was all so new.
He simply said, "There's big black kuris
towing land canoes!"

Anyway, no one believed him.
Said, "He's telling lies,"
and the kids rode on the pigs, and laughed,
and laughed until they cried!

Chapter 5:

# Ruatara's Biscuits

Our warrior turned the ladies' heads
but this man's heart was taken.
Miki made his knees go weak
but let's not get mistaken.

She couldn't keep her mind off him,
so what this girl would do
while hunky spunky was at sea,
she'd write a song or two.

She wrote love songs and let me tell you
those songs made a hit.
She'd sing one and the kids would listen
then start singing it!

After time even the blokes
who heard her latest song
would find themselves humming the tune
and singing right along.

When Ruatara left Australia
heading over here,
Marsden met another chief
just travelling back there.

"Ruatara has a wife, right?
How's she getting on?"
The young chief put his head back,
smiled, and then sang Miki's song.

Miki was the daughter
of the chief at Waitangi.
Wairaki was so proud of her
as daddies tend to be.

Miki had more songs to write
and now her love was back.
This was the man she wrote about.
She'd write another track!

No biscuits here, nor bakeries.
We didn't grow the wheat,
so Ruatara brought back seeds
and six chiefs said, "That's neat!

But what is wheat? How does it taste?
Please give us some to grow."
Our warrior said he'd give them seeds
so they could take them home.

He showed them how and when to plant
then off they went back home.
He told them, "Leave it in the ground
till it is fully grown."

But as it grew some couldn't wait;
they pulled it up to see.
"There's no wheat on the bottom. Look!
He's made a fool of me."

Before their crops were fully grown
five chiefs ripped them out.
Then they burned the rest of it
before the lad found out.

"Hey, boy! There's no wheat under there.
There's no wheat to be found."
But wheat grows at the top of plants,
spuds grow underground.

Now Hongi said, "I kept my crop.
See, it is fully grown."
So the lad made biscuits from that wheat
and man, did those chiefs moan!

"What have we done? Where's our biscuits?
Oh, have we burned our bread?
We wanted to look very smart.
Now we look dumb instead."

The moral here is very clear:
we all have much to learn.
These chiefs were fine intelligent men,
and they had brains to burn.

But we don't know what we don't know
and there is no exception.
These men were fooled by what they knew.
How's that for deception!

Chapter 6:

# Samuel's Sailing Ship

Many times Samuel tried
to send his friend some stuff:
scissors, nails, fishhooks, scales,
but, oh man! It was tough.

Many times he couldn't trust
the captains of the ships.
Mostly when they got the stuff
they just sailed off with it.

Samuel saw a ship for sale
although it wasn't big,
he took out all his cash that day
and bought himself a brig.

The *Active* was its proper name
and it was kinda stark
but it would be historic—
it would soon get called "*The Ark!*"

He sent it to New Zealand
with a captain he could trust,
and a teacher, and a builder,
and some tools that had no rust.

A flour mill and other stuff
like sugar, flour and cheese,
a chest filled up with clothing
and some axes, hoes and seeds.

An order in his papers
to the captain, Marsden wrote,
"Make sure that on the Sabbath
all work ceases on the boat,

'cause God says it's important
and men need a day of rest."
You know, when Maori found that out
they thought it was the best.

One whole day off from work a week?
They hardly could believe it.
They worked like stink all days each week.
"This God's way? We receive it."

Samuel Marsden was "The Man!"
They couldn't wait to meet him
and when the boat sailed back to Oz
Ruatara went to greet him.

He'd bring his dear friend back with him
no matter what the weather.
His dearest friend, the Pakeha.
They'd both sail back together.

A new appointed captain
for the voyage was the plan.
Ena's great great grandad,
Thomas Hansen was the man.

As Samuel Marsden prayed to God
to show him what to do
excitement grew inside him,
this was God's plan and he knew.

There were tribes up in the north,
the east, the south, and in the west.
Sam had heaps of Maori friends
but what about the rest?

What if one tribe presupposed
he was an enemy?
All these thoughts went through his head.
He'd have to wait and see!

## Chapter 7

# The 'Ark's' Voyage

This was it! The voyage
Sam had dreamed about for years.
When captain shouted, "Cast off!"
he was fighting back the tears.

Giving thanks to God
'cause that's the perfect place to start,
he felt like he was going home
with good news on his heart.

Ruatara won the hearts
of many Pakeha.
For Maori that was easy
'cause it's just the way they are.

Polite and with a twinkle,
they were strong and full of fun.
Strongest on the whaling boats
and fit from where they'd come.

Someone gave the lad a horse—
it was a warrior's treasure!
The first horse ever to our shores—
its worth you couldn't measure.

Before they put the horse on board
they had to stow the cattle,
the bull, some goats, some pigs and dogs,
the poultry and some chattels.

Samuel took another mare,
a stallion and some cats
and sheep, which all would eat and poo.
Now try to picture that!

The little ship with all its zoo,
it settled in the bay.
And then, with tears and moos and clucks
the wee ship sailed away.

The boat that Samuel Marsden bought
not long ago so stark
was heading off to change a world
resembling 'Noah's Ark!'

## Chapter 8:
# The Zoo Arrives

"Land Ahoy!" called out the boy
as New Zealand came in view.
The captain noticed rocks ahead
and knew just what to do.

He said to Ruatara,
"Take the wheel, the ship is yours.
You know every rock that's here,
so guide us to your shores."

3pm, Te Puna Bay.
Ruatara, he was home.
Samuel caught the warrior's smile.
This time not alone!

The ship's longboats lowered
for the animals to ride.
To get to shore you had to row
with a cow on either side.

Cows and pigs and goats afloat
with chickens, cats and sheep.
With all that noise the girls and boys
were lined up on the beach.

Very soon the zoo was beached.
Imagine what a sight.
Free at last, one cow took off
and everyone took flight!

Women grabbed the kids
and men their mates and disappeared.
They hadn't seen a cow before
and Poof...!  The place was cleared.

Finally the cow was caught
and everyone returned.
Then the stallion came ashore
and all the heads were turned.

Three monsters stood upon the land
with muscles rippling proud.
Samuel mounted one of them.
A hush fell on the crowd.

The horse it thundered down the beach.
The man and beast were one.
In broad daylight, a stunning sight!
Majestic in the sun.

Now to the cat. Yeah, what is that?
With fur our Lord did coat her.
"Now just be gentle, softly stroke,
shhh... listen... *(purrrrr).*  There's the motor!"

The goat, it is the lawnmower
to keep the land in trim.
The pig, the waste disposal
and we all knew about him.

But what's that bag under the cow?
Yeah, what's that all about?
"See those handles?  Squeeze and pull
and then drink what comes out!"

The cow eats grass, turns it to milk—
now there's a fairy tale.
Better than turning straw to gold.
This treasure will not fail.

Cow keeps eating, grass keeps growing,
milk keeps coming out.
"Mr Marsden, this is magic!"
"Mmm... that's what God's about!"

Trying to explain to folks
the chooks that Samuel got 'em.
Explaining how we eat the eggs
that plopped out of their bottom.

The horse, of course, it was the prize.
'Till now you'd walk or paddle.
The horse was perfect, made for us
to climb aboard and straddle.

Ruatara rode with pride
but always he would share.
In Oz they used the saddle seat
but here we'd ride it bare.

"All these things God made for us,"
Mr Marsden he would say.
We liked the God who made all this.
We'd hear more Christmas Day.

## Chapter 9

# NZ's First Christmas
# -25th December 1814

Ruatara dragged canoes
some distance up the sand.
He turned them upside down
and everybody gave a hand.

They made the outside look like church
'cept better – it was neat!
The canoes that now were upside down
provided guests a seat.

The sky was very blue and clear
that Christmas Monday morn
and for Sam and Ruatara
a dream was being born.

Marsden had been humbly
helping Maori twenty years
and now he wanted them to know
his heart, his love, his tears!

Everyone had gathered
and he started with a song.
Maori all love music
so they all sang right along.

Then he took a verse
from the Bible, chapter two,
Luke's Gospel says,
"Glad tidings of great joy for me and you."

Christmas time was new to us.
God, He had a son.
He sent him to be born a man!
Now that freaked everyone.

Why on earth would God do that?
His Son, a human! Why?
'Cause without becoming human,
well, God's Son could never die.

Wait a minute! Why do that?
Why would God want to die?
It's the only way that we could live forever—
that is why!

I know He loves us, seen the horse
and all the other stuff
but coming here so he could die
to save us? That is rough!

How come God loves us that much
when we didn't love Him back?
That's the Good News, He can't help it.
We're whanau (family). That's a fact!

Ruatara seemed to know
about this Jesus man.
He wanted us to have the message
planted in our land.

So Christmas was the day
to celebrate this Jesus' birth
and here forever after,
God has shown us what we're worth.

"The 'God Book' must be printed
in our land for everyone."
So 'Te Rongopai e Ruka'  (The Gospel of Luke)
is the first book in our tongue.

# PART 2:

# The Message

## Chapter 10

# Te Waharoa
## - Slave boy to Mighty Chief

Around this time but further south
in the mighty Waikato,
there was a small tribe living there
wedged between their foes.

Taiporutu was the chief
of the Ngati-Hauā then
before they moved from Cambridge
to the flat lands nearer Thames.

A chief in the Waikato
he was tough and he was strong,
but his biggest fight was still to come
and that would not be long.

His brother's wife was 'hapu' (pregnant)
and her baby soon would come.
With 'Uncle' Taiporutu
celebrations would be fun.

Taiporutu liked to fight,
his men were men of valour,
but he didn't listen to his wife....
It caused his death, poor fella!

She didn't want him going off
to a Taranaki pa.
Things were a mess there in the west
and she could lose her star!

"It's time to stop your fighting, dear.
You shouldn't be so wild.
You're about to be an uncle.
Just think about that child!"

"Yeah, yeah!" he said, "I'll settle down.
Just give me one more fight."
But the boys out west were very tough
and they put out his light.

They hung his body on the gate,
the gateway to the pa.
He should have listened to his wife
'cause she knew best by far!

'Te Waharoa' was the name
they called the baby boy.
Born now after his uncle's death,
which took away much joy.

His name means 'gateway' to the pa,
so no one would forget
the waste that comes from fighting
and the pain of man's regret.

The boy was only two years old
when Pango came to town.
He came from Rotorua.
The Arawa were his crown.

He fought the Ngati-Hauā men
and won the fight that day;
captured the small boy and his mum
and carried them away.

Slaving for the Arawa,
that's how the boy grew up.
Doing all the hardest jobs
he learned to 'suck it up!'

He learned he must have patience
and not ever lose his cool.
For slaves there was no second chance,
no second chance at all.

"Better to control yourself
than an army full of guys.
Patience stands you in good stead
a patient man is wise."

It was King Solomon wrote that once;
the richest, wisest king.
So the slave learned to control himself
more than anything.

'Nobody knows why but'... here goes...
they set the young slave free!
They kept his mum, but just for fun
they set him loose—whoopee!

In time they would regret that move
'cause he had watched them train.
He knew their ways, he knew their plays
and now **free** in the rain!

Where would he go at just nineteen?
Would his people have him back?
They hadn't seen him since he's two,
but spunk he didn't lack.

Within three years he had command,
his 'mana' was that strong.
He bore himself majestically.
It didn't take too long

'till Ngati-Hauā realized
that he had what it takes
to be the leader of the tribe.
Wow, 'ey?   What a break!

He found his love, they had two sons,
one called Tarapipipi.
This boy God destined to grow up
to set his people free.

Free from the hurts and from the hate,
from bloodshed and from war.
They'd never had what he would bring;
things God had in store!

Now let's get right back into it,
that's if you like adventures
with wonders, wits and warriors
and winning in the trenches.

A trench is just a big long ditch
and here they were effective.
Waikato river brings the fog
which helps things get deceptive.

Te Waharoa learned his skills
while living with the Arawa,
but no one guessed how good he was,
his wits they knew no barrier.

Two tribes teamed up to come
and beat the cheese out of this man.
But had they known how good he was
they would have thought again.

The fog had set in thick that day
and Te Waharoa smiled,
"I've waited all my life for this
since I was just a child!"

"Come out and face us," the tribes yelled,
"you couldn't fight our auntie.
We say your chief is useless.
Well?  Can he fight or can't he?"

Our young chief whispered, "Don't be dumb.
Just go and get the gear.
We'll dig a trench across the pa,
starting over here."

Te Waharoa had a plan
and all his people knew
he was well trained; he would explain
the best thing they could do.

Hid by the fog they dug the ditch
while enemies kept screaming.
"Now ladies start the fires up
and get some food on steaming....

Cook enough for two whole days
and tell us when it's ready.
Don't worry about all their noise.
They won't make me unsteady."

The ladies cooked, the warriors dug
and everyone kept silent.
The yelling and the screaming
through the fog got very violent.

"Noise won't hurt you, carry on,"
the chieftain's words were soothing.
"They'll wear themselves out soon enough
but let's just keep on moving."

When all was done and food was cooked
he turned then to the children,
"Tie the dogs up—down the back—
not far so we can hear them.

Climb in the trench, and bring the food.
We'll hide and keep real silent.
Now not one word! Upon your life!
These tribes might get real violent."

Quiet in the ditch they sat
with spears all at the ready.
The fog, the silence, the fires out,
soon it got really heady.

After time the tribal chiefs
were puzzled what to think.
The dogs, now hungry, barked for food
and something just to drink.

"There's no fires! They've run away!
and left their dogs behind.
What a pack of wusses.
Come, let's see what we can find.

We'll take their stuff away and then
we'll ransack their whole pa
and Aotearoa will know
how chicken these blokes are."

Laying down their weapons
they all walked in through the gate.
Te Waharoa passed the whisper,
"Wait, not yet, just wait....

Wait until you see the little
white bits in their eyes."
Then suddenly, WHAM! BAM!
The place erupted to the skies!

The biggest fright recorded
in the history of our land
was when Te Waharoa stood
to fight there with his men.

It was no contest, both tribes fled—
ran half way to forever.
So did they come to fight again?
Not on your life! Nah! **NEVER**!

Te Waharoa, famous now,
'the chief who whipped them all,'
was sitting one day listening
to a Tui bird's bright call.

He'd heard that further up the north
the fighting seemed to stop.
"What is it we don't have down here
that they've got up the top?

What have they got that's different
I should send someone to look."
It wasn't long till he was told
"It's, cause of the 'God Book'!"

"What is the 'God Book'?  What is that?
Get them to bring it here.
I'm tired of fighting all the time
and families live in fear."

He heard about the mission
up near Ruatara's pa.
He'd heard of Samuel Marsden,
the Pommie Pakeha.

But what intrigued his curious mind,
"How could you change man's heart?"
And if this 'God Book' had the key,
then that's the place to start.

Chapter 11:

# Tarore and Ngakuku

"Hey Tarore! Put that spear down.
Don't hold it up that way.
A girl could slip and fall on it
and that would end her days.

Now how's your reading coming on?
I saw it in the sand.
Your teacher drawing letters
with a stick held in his hand.

Where is the 'God Book' that you took
to read down by the river?
I hope you kept it very safe
I only had one to give ya!"

She pointed to the small kit bag
on a flax chord 'round her neck,
"See this is where I keep it Dad,
it's safe as you can get!

Isn't it exciting Dad?
I've watched you learning too.
God's words they make me happy.
Do they do the same to you?"

Her dad, Ngakuku, was the chief
at the Okauia Pa.
He smiled down at his princess,
"Yes, but you read best by far."

She read the words with passion
as twelve year olds can do.
The people loved to hear her read;
to them it was all new.

Not just the way she spoke the words
but what was in the book.
Miracles were taking place
and 'Pip,' he came to look.

Tarapipipi was his name
and we call him 'Pip' for short.
The great chief's son just had to read;
he wanted to be taught.

Te Waharoa's nephew said,
"Count me in this too!"
So both Ngakuku and his cousin 'Pip'
were learning something new.

'Maori' was the language
but it wasn't written down.
No one here could read or write
'till missionaries came to town.

We didn't have the text book
'till the 'God Book' came along,
and we didn't have a writing
so we couldn't spell it wrong!

The whalers, traders and gun runners,
some of them could read
but they didn't care or give a toss
to help our moral creed.

They would teach us other stuff
like how to shoot a gun
and drink the 'fire water,'
which would make a wise man dumb!

But the missionaries who lived with us
came here because they cared.
It must have been real rough for them.
Sometimes they'd be scared.

Imagine leaving England
to come live here in the bush.
The closest shop? Australia,
so you couldn't be a wus.

When Te Waharoa sent
for missionaries to come,
his people got excited
'cause they'd not seen one—not one!

"What is a missionary?" they asked.
The messenger wasn't sure.
"They don't wear sailors' clothes
or carry guns and that's for sure.

White ladies glide in big long skirts—
the gliding looks real neat.
Their dresses go down to the ground...
they might have wheels, not feet!

The men are kind and don't have guns
and neither 'fire water.'
That stuff will make you stupid.
If you don't know that, you oughta!"

The missionaries arrived
from the Paihia mission station.
They'd come from half way 'round the world
to our little nation.

Mr Wilson, Mr Brown,
and both their families,
they fitted in as if
they hadn't come from overseas.

They spoke our language when they came;
they learned it in the north.
At first it did seem strange that
from their tongues our words came forth.

"Here's a hammer, hold this end
then grab that tiny spear.
Hold the sharp end on the wood,
now hit the top right there!

That tiny spear is called a nail.
The nail goes through the wood,
so bang those two together, yep!
You did that very good!"

The people had not seen a saw
before they saw the saw,
but when they saw the saw they saw
they saw what it was for.

They sawed the wood, they got the nails,
they built the mission house,
and when they saw the chisel,
well now, that was something else!

Shovels, axes, pots and pans,
and spades and ploughs and seeds.
The lantern made the night daylight,
and hoes pulled out the weeds.

Blankets, hats, shoes and mats
and beads just for the girls.
Te Waharoa shared the gifts
from the missionaries' world.

The 'God Book' that Ngakuku got
he shared it with his girl.
They both were learning how to read.
Its words would change their world.

## Chapter 12

# The Message of the 'God Book'

After hunting through the day
the warriors would relax.
Someone would be given charge
to peel or skin the catch.

To pluck a duck or wipe off muck
from slimy, greasy eels.
The women were the best of cooks!
They made the yummy meals.

The kai was cooked, out came the Book
as all sat 'round the flames.
Tarore, she began to read
and the children stopped their games.

The fire cracked, then silence fell,
they waited for the words.
She took a big deep breath
making sure she would get heard.

"Listen all of you!" she read,
"Love your enemies!"
"Nah!  What? Don't make it up!
Hey girl, you read it properly."

"I'm reading just what God says here.
He says we shouldn't fight.
Maybe God who made the world
is wrong and we are right!

These are the words from God," she said,
"exactly what He says."
"Ok, read on. God can't be wrong
but he sure has strange ways."

"Do good to those who hate you."
Now that is something new.
The warriors were stunned by that
and maybe you are too!

"Pray for the happiness of people
when they're cursing you.
Implore God's blessings on the ones
who try to hurt you too."

"What? Wait up! That can't be right,
what can God be thinking?"
But Tarore just kept reading on
her eyes were hardly blinking.

"If someone slaps you on one cheek,
let him slap the other too."
"WHAT?" the warrior's voice rang out,
"Hey, that's not what we do!

If someone slapped me on the face,
he'd better start to run.
Well, he might slap me with his hand
but I will use a gun!"

The tribe was all in shock at what
the 'God Book' had to say,
but never mind, our girl read on.
She let them know Gods way.

"Give what you have to anyone
if it's something that they lack.
When things are taken from you
don't try to get them back.

Love your foes, do good to them,
and lend your stuff to them.
Don't get worried by the fact
they won't repay again.

Then your reward from heaven
will be very, very great,
'cause you'll be acting like God's sons."
(Just think if **God's** your mate!)

"Treat others simply how you'd want
 the others to treat you,
for if you give then you will get!
That's what God promised you."

As she read the stories
of Jesus and his men,
the warriors would ask at times
to read that bit again.

God's way, it was so different
from the utu and the war.
His way of love was powerful.
They wanted to hear more.

A miracle was happening
in Tarore's little heart.
She read and read the 'God Book'
and she now knew every part.

She knew that God won't ask us
to do things He doesn't do,
so when He loves His enemies,
He must love me and you.

Even ones who hate Him,
He still does the kind things to.
'Love' is just the spelling
but it means 'kind things you do!'

The power of Love was working.
She felt God's amazing grace.
She knew that Jesus loved her
and He died to take her place.

Her dad, Ngakuku, felt the same
and on the self same day
they both asked different missionaries
to help them now to pray.

A warrior, the great chief's son,
had also felt God's touch
and he got down on both his knees
and thanked the Lord so much.

Tarapipipi, 'Pip' for short,
accepted God's free gift.
A life with **full forgiveness**
Jesus paid the price for it!

Chapter 13:
# The Big Move

Te Waharoa fought a chief
in hand to hand combat.
The chief from Rotorua tried
to get the best of that.

"Don't fight!" Te Waharoa said,
"Let's live in peace instead."
But the other chief just wouldn't stop
so he wound up dead instead.

Te Waharoa won the fight
but got wounded in the thigh.
His son, Tarapipipi said,
"The price of war's too high.

Dad, let me build a pa
that will be a pa of peace
where we won't carry weapons
and where killing men will cease."

"I told that chief; he wouldn't stop."
Our chief was heard to say,
"This fighting is ridiculous
I think we'll move away."

Rotorua's raiding parties
from the tribes down there
often came into the swamps
to raid the place up here.

Wooden fences of the pa
were no match for a gun.
Te Waharoa thought it best
to just shift everyone.

The children sensed adventure;
the decision it was done.
They'd walk across the Kaimai Range
all through the bush—that's fun!

Ngakuku would go with them
and two other Christian men
to the big pa at Tauranga.
They'd all be safer then.

The children would be first to leave;
they took the chairs and table.
The older boys, they carried those
'cause older boys are able.

Climbing through the swamps and bush,
you know, that wasn't easy.
The muck it stuck all over things
and made the table greasy.

Tarore grabbed her brother close.
He was only four.
They missed their mummy since she died
and now they missed her more.

She tried a while to carry him.
He liked it on her back,
just like Daddy carried him
but not as high as that.

"I think I'll put you down now.
You are strong and you can climb."
She tried to make him feel grown up.
She did that all the time.

The time he liked the best
was when she put him on the horse.
Twenty-one children all took turns.
They liked that best of course.

When the horses first arrived,
the children stared and stared... and **stared**!
They thought the horse might eat them.
Some ran away real scared.

But Mr Flatt, he fixed all that.
He was the one who brought them.
Both horses were trained to be good
and he's the one who taught them.

They sang and laughed, then suddenly
they heard a rushing sound.
Someone cried, "Hey look up there!"
And guess what they had found?

A waterfall in two great leaps,
five hundred feet in height.
Beside it stood a raupo hut
where they would camp the night.

These children from the swamp
had never seen a sight like this.
Tarore picked her brother up
and gave a little kiss,

"God is clever, don't you think?"
She smiled at his wide eyes.
It was a stunning place to be,
a wonderful surprise.

Waiere falls we call the place.
It still looks just the same
but something happened there that night
that history was to claim.

The boys took off to gather ferns
for beds inside the hut,
and Mr Flatt, he pitched a tent
to put in all the stuff.

It was the 19th of October 1836.
A fire would be needed
so the children gathered sticks.

They lit a fire and cooked some kai
and then sat down to eat.
After all pukus were full
Tarore had a treat.

The 'God Book' had great stories
about Jesus and his men.
They'd heard the stories many times
but loved to hear again.

The story that she read that night
was Luke 8:22.
Jesus' men were petrified
and didn't know what to do.

They'd gone out fishing in the boat
to sail across the lake.
Jesus lay down for a nap
but they were wide awake.

The clouds grew dark, the wind blew up
and soon it was a storm.
The biggest storm they'd ever seen
and nothing like the norm.

The waves began to crash on board.
The boat began to shudder.
The sea too strong, they fought so long
to hold onto the rudder.

"Look out! Look out! Or we'll fall out!"
is what they all were thinking.
Then someone screamed in Jesus' ear,
"LORD WAKE UP! WE'RE SINKING!"

It didn't seem to faze Him.
He just stood to wipe His eyes.
The waves were just like mountains
but He didn't look surprised.

With one command Jesus spoke.
He called out, "PEACE... BE STILL!"
Instantly the storm it stopped,
it just obeyed His will.

The men were stunned
it was so still, as calm as you can get.
Then Jesus asked them, "Where's your faith?"
But it hadn't sunk in yet.

"Who is this man?" they asked around,
"that winds and waves obey?"
They never would forget God's power
He showed them on that day.

She stopped the reading for the night
though some they wanted more.
The raupo hut felt cosy
with the fern down on the floor.

A puzzled look came on her face.
She turned then to her dad
and quietly she said to him,
"E Pa (O Daddy) it is sad.

Jesus friends should not have feared
when they were in the storm
'cause Jesus, He was with them."
Then she lay down snug and warm.

Ngakuku would, in days to come,
remember what she said.
He thought about her trust in God.
He bent and kissed her head.

# Chapter 14:
# The Raiding Party

A Rotorua raiding band
from the Arawa Marae,
were out for trouble on that night,
saw smoke rise in the sky.

"That must be traders at the falls.
Let's all sneak up on them.
We'll kill them and we'll have their guns
then sneak back home again."

Small bands of well-trained warriors—
'raiding parties' they were called.
I call them 'raiding ratbags'
'cause they did no good at all.

Parties are for birthdays
and birthdays are for fun
but these men were for mischief,
so look out 'cause here they come!

These warriors could walk barefoot,
through bush without one sound.
You could never hear them come
or know they were around.

The noise that night from the waterfalls
blocked out any sound.
The children, they had no idea
these killers were around.

Only a sound above the noise
of the water falling down
could wake the children from their sleep
to warn them someone's round.

Quietly the braves edged close.
They could easily kill them all
not knowing they were children,
not knowing that at all.

Uira led them closer.
He could hear the waters fall
though none of them could see a thing—
it was pitch black after all.

Uira was an Arawa chief.
Right now he felt so strong
and he was sure he'd kill them all,
but he was very wrong.

One thing this chief had never seen,
he'd never seen a horse
and there were two tied to a tree
in front of him, of course.

It was real dark, as black as pitch.
The time to fight was near.
Tied to the tree he couldn't see
was something he would fear.

He walked, of course, into a horse
and let out such a **_SCREAM_**
so loud it woke the children up!
Those monsters looked real mean!

The children of the Ngati-Hauā,
they were trained well too
to run away at times like this.
They knew just what to do.

They rushed out of the hut's far door
and ran into the night,
but there were three who couldn't see
and didn't do it right.

They ran together through the door,
the front door of the hut,
into the arms of Uira!
He picked Tarore up.

His men, they let the others go
when they saw all the stuff.
The other girls ran fast away,
the warriors mucked that up!

In the dark Ngakuku thought
the children all were safe.
They all had heard Uira's scream
and found a hiding place.

Mr Flatt, just think of that,
he went back for the horse.
He managed to free both of them
and sneak back up the course.

Uira held the struggling girl.
She was no match for him.
She struggled but it was no use
and fear was setting in.

"Ngakuku! Daddy!" she called out,
then suddenly a thought!
Jesus is in this boat with me,
where is the book I brought?

Her flailing hands suddenly caught
the flax kit with the book.
Her stormy screaming suddenly stopped.
Uira, stunned, just looked!

Instantly a look of peace
and joy lit up her face.
As she died, "Ihu! (Jesus)" she cried
and went to Jesus' place.

Uira had not ever seen
a person die that way.
It was like someone reached inside
and took her fear away.

The peace that shone from her sweet face
he never would forget
and from that day this moment
is the one that he'd regret.

"What is in the flax kit here
that removed her fear to die?"
He ripped it from around her neck,
desperate to find why.

He ran as fast as he could run.
One thing was very clear.
The girl who died was filled with peace;
he was filled with fear.

He reached into the kit at home
and inside found the book.
He opened up its pages
and he took a closer look.

"Aaargh! This is simply nothing!
What is this anyway?"
He threw it on his whare floor
but couldn't turn away.

He couldn't get the picture
of Tarore from his mind.
He picked the strange thing off the floor,
"There's something here to find!"

The chieftain's daughter he had killed
had something that was new.
Why did she call out 'Jesus'?  (Ihu)
That's a name he never knew.

This strange thing from the flax kit,
he knew it held the key
so he would carry it close to him
and one day he would see.

## Chapter 15

# Utu Stops Here!

Ngakuku heard Tarore's screams
echo through the hills.
He turned and raced with all his pace
to find her lying still.

Her killer gone into the night,
he bowed his head in pain.
The thought he had was not revenge
but returning home again.

His heart was breaking as he bent
to lift her off the ground.
It was fifteen kilometres in his arms
to carry her back down.

His father heart felt ripped apart.
Each step was just a blur,
"Why did she die and not me, Lord?
Why not me instead of her?"

He longed to speak to Mr Brown,
the missionary, his friend,
the one who'd brought the 'God Book',
that she'd carried to the end.

He laid her body gently down
when he reached the marae.
Ngakuku was not comforted
when he heard the people cry.

They cried out for revenge
but that was nowhere on his mind.
"Was his girl in heaven?"
was the truth that he must find.

"Ngakuku, come." said Mr Brown,
"Don't heed their bad behaviour.
Some don't know of God's great love.
Let's hear Tarore's Saviour."

He opened up the Bible,
the 'God Book' on his knee
and seated there on that wood box
he helped Ngakuku see.

He read...
'Let not your heart be troubled,
do not let it be afraid.
My Father's house has many rooms,
there's one for you I've made.'

"Tarore's safe in her heavenly home,
of that you can be sure.
She loved the Lord Jesus Christ
but Chief, **He loved her more.**

Remember how she treasured His book
and shared His love around?
She found God's power in His words,
now she's on heaven's ground."

"My heart is calm," Ngakuku said,
"as Jesus calmed the sea.
`Peace! Be still! I am with you.'
That's what He says to me.

There'll be no fighting over her.
People put down your spears.
We will see what God will do,
but **UTU STOPS**... right here!

Tarore read God's Book to us,
so we know what God says.
**'Forgiveness and not Utu**,'
so that starts right here... TODAY!"

The tribe stood silent in their shock
but thinking in their head,
"How can our chief forgive them
and not get revenge instead?"

Their chief they knew was fearless
and was not afraid to fight
but something stronger than revenge
was in his eyes tonight.

"No chieftain in our land does this...
forgive and not pay back!"
But Ngakuku said, "**NO UTU!**"
And that, my friends, was that!

He thought of his girl often,
in his mind he'd see her face.
Now she was safe with Jesus,
in His boat and at His place.

So he would trust in God as chief
just as his girl had done
and someday God would show him why,
and that day soon would come.

Chapter 16:
# The Slave: Ripahau

No one knows why but up north
another slave set free
was told by those who'd captured him,
"Go find the missionaries."

They told him, "In Paihia
God's men will give you kai
and get you started on your way
back down to your marae."

He found the mission station
and he said, "I'm Ripahau.
I've been a slave for many years.
I've just been freed right now!"

They gave him food, looked after him,
and then taught him to read.
They could not know the harvest
that would come from those few seeds.

He took with him some pages
of a prayer book that they gave.
The children came to see him off,
their fellow student waved.

He'd been through much pain in his life,
he'd shared that on the mat.
His life of slavery left it's marks,
though love could change all that.

But he had something splendid
he could take home to his tribe.
He'd show them how to read and write
and he felt great inside.

A slave set free and coming home
with a gift for everyone.
His heart was lightened by the thought,
"Otaki, here I come!"

There was no highway number one
or GPS or such.
The journey was a dangerous one
but it didn't matter much.

See, he was free and he could read
and he could write stuff down,
so he could trade by teaching folks
who knew their way around.

With his skill he now could help
other people learn,
so as he travelled he helped them
and they helped him in turn.

The journey took a long time
but he was doing well.
He came to Rotorua
and he smelled an awful smell.

The steam from hot pools, geysers
and hot mud was plain to see,
and the smell of sulphur
was like rotten eggs to you and me.

Right here a miracle took place,
a miracle God planned.
He bumped into a man who held
the 'God Book' in his hand.

"Watch out!" Uira said,
"Don't you know just who I am?"
But Ripahau was staring
at the 'God Book' in his hand.

"Where did you get that 'God Book'?
Have the Christian men been here?"

"I took it from a girl I killed
and that's the truth... I swear!

Why? Do you know what this is?"
Uira asked the man.

"Could I see it? Pass it here."
Wow! Can you see God's plan?

Imagine what would be the chance
that these two men would meet
to open up that 'God Book'
on a Rotorua Street.

## Chapter 17

# The Miracle of Forgiveness



Ripahau looked inside
the cover of the book.
"Ngakuku," he read out loud.
Uira, he just shook.

"Where? Where? Where? He's not in there.
Don't tell me he could fit."

"No, here's his NAME," said Ripahau,
"and I'm just reading it."

"How'd you do that? What is reading?
I don't understand.
That thing has troubled me so long,
that thing there in your hand."

Uira told his story of Tarore,
how she died.
He couldn't get her from his mind
and wanted to know why.

"She kept this in a kit bag
round her neck," Uira cried,
"and when she held it she lit up
with peace from deep inside."

"I want to find out what's inside
this strange thing that I took,
and if you know please show me.
You just called it the 'God Book'."

Ripahau felt useful
like he hadn't felt in years.
Here was a mighty chieftain
telling Ripahau his fears.

*"What is happening in my life?"*
he wondered on the street,
*"What a strange coincidence
that him and I should meet."*

"I've come from high up in the north,
I journey on my own.
I'm only half way to my tribe,
I must keep going home."

"Stay here a while, teach me to read
and I will feed you well.

I'll look after you myself
and don't worry 'bout the smell....

You soon get used to that round here—
the steam helps cook the kai.
The hot pools you can rest in,
now there's some reasons why."

Ripahau thought, "*He'll feed me well,*
*so maybe I could stay.*
*The hot springs in the winter*
*will wash my aches away....*

*I'd get to teach a chief to read and write.*
*That's one, two, three.*
*Three reasons I should stay a while!*
*Seems pretty good to me!*"

"Ok we have a deal," he said,
but soon as you can read
I must be heading on my way."
And so began the deed.

They read the book together
and God's way was plain to see,
the story of how Jesus paid
the price to set men free.

It all was there, it all was clear
and Uira, he found out
that's why Tarore had such peace,
that's what it's all about.

But as they read through all the book
Uira, he could tell
that Ripahau was struggling
with the truth he knew so well.

He didn't like to read some parts,
he sort of made it plain,
especially when Uira asked,
"Hey, read that bit again?"

"You don't believe in this my friend,"
Uira asked, "Do you?
You don't believe what God has done.
That Jesus died for you?"

Ripahau looked angry now,
"I don't," he said, "I won't."
"How come you won't believe?"
"I don't know why, but I just don't!"

"I think it's cause your heart is dark
with anger and with hate
against the tribe that hurt you
and made you become their slave.

God's book speaks of forgiving,
says to love your enemies.
Why don't you just try doing that,
forgive and then believe!

I want to believe this for myself,
but one thing I must do.
I first must cross the Kaimai Range
and visit Ngakuku.

I must ask his forgiveness
for taking his child's life.
His daughter, she believed God's love,
I saw it in her eyes.

If he kills me, I'll be dead
and I'll have paid my price.
If he forgives and spares my life,
I'll follow Jesus Christ."

Ripahau had taught him well.
Uira he could read.
This was the germination
of Paihia's mission seed.

Both men had kept the deal they made
and yes, that task was done.
Now they would go their separate ways
so greater things could come.

Ripahau would head down south,
walking back to home
but Uira laid his weapons down
and headed off alone.

He walked and thought of that dark night
that now had changed his life.
The words from God had changed his heart
to do the way that's right.

Just think about what happened next.
Remember Ngakuku's words,
"We will see what God will do!"
Well, heaven must have heard.

"A warrior's coming," someone cried,
"and he is all alone.
He has no weapons, I am sure.
Looks like he's coming home!"

Let's stop here for a moment
and take a closer look.
Uira is about to die
and that could end our book!

If there is not a miracle,
he is about to die.
There is no coming back from this
and here's the reason why.

He killed the precious daughter
of the chief he's come to see.
He has no weapon!  He's alone!
Just check our History!

He is about to do something
that no-one's ever done
with a thousand years of 'Utu'
screaming, "He's the guilty one!"

Uira had the strangest peace
this could be his last day.
But he must find if God is real.
He'd find it out this way.

A stranger, he was welcomed in
and asked from where he'd come.
"I must see chief Ngakuku
before I speak to anyone."

The tribe all gathered 'round him
then Ngakuku was called out.
"What can I do for you my friend?
What is this all about?"

Now this was not an easy thing
Uira had to do,
and if he died, he knew he'd tried.
"Lord help me see this through."

"Sir, I am from the Arawa,
I'm the one they call Uira.
I am sorry for all the pain you bear.
It was me who killed your daughter."

The people hushed in total shock.
How could this ever be?
"I know your daughter died in peace
I beg you, please forgive me."

The tribe, they listened, still in shock.
Uira told his story.
Ngakuku smiled... there'd be no trial.
This moment is for God's Glory!

That moment seemed like time stood still
and heaven held its breath....
What would change our nation
was the thing that happened next.

He held his daughter's killer close
and gave forgiveness freely.
They both embraced... **amazing grace!**
Believe me, that's not easy!

From hurt, from pain and guilt and shame,
from darkness and frustration,
two hearts were free, as clean can be.
This God could heal our nation!

Shockwaves rang throughout the land.
Forgiveness had God's power.
This deed began to heal our land.
**Our country's finest hour.**

Chapter 18:

# The Fire Spreads

Uira went back to his home,
where missionaries now came.
He knew for sure God's way is true
and others learned the same.

Alive, Uira was the proof
the 'God Book' way is best.
The truth that God would honour
had been really put to test.

Ngakuku began to journey
going east from where he lived,
and everywhere the tribes received
the message he would give.

Although the news had travelled,
now they heard it face to face.
The story of Tarore helped them
understand God's grace.

The power of forgiveness
spread like fire through the trees,
and everywhere the message went
people bowed their knees.

Nothing has more power
than forgiving from the heart.
God lit the spark at the cross of Christ,
now Tarore played her part.

Ngakuku fanned the growing flames
when Uira came to town.
Now down the East Coast of our land
that fire was spreading 'round.

# PART 3:

# The Peacemaker

## Chapter 19

# The Journey South

Let's tell you about Ripahau.
What happened now to him?
Well, he set out for Otaki.
He walked, he didn't swim.

Otaki is a long way down
from Rotorua south.
Imagine walking all that way.
Whew! That would wear you out.

But this man Ripahau was fit,
handsome, strong and trim.
For us to climb a cliff
was like for him a biscuit tin.

No fat fast foods or lollies,
and no cars, not even roads.
No trailers and no roof racks.
You just had to carry loads.

No need for gyms to get you slim
'cause life took care of that.
Just walk down to Otaki overland.
Yeah! Goodbye fat!

Ripahau could not be sure
they'd welcome his return,
but he was sure that he could teach
what most folks want to learn.

Especially reading and of course
learning to write stuff down.
He saw the sea in front of him—
next stop, Otaki town!

## Chapter 20

# Katu and Te Whiwhi

'Te Rauparaha.' Those two words
brought fear throughout the south.
Some blokes they make a lot of show
but they just have big mouths.

Not this chief though, he had the 'goods',
or the 'bads' to back it up.
No one dared to mess with him.
Nah! He was very tough!

The ones who lived in fear of him
were tribes much further south.
The South Island was beautiful
but not when he's about.

He built the biggest, flashest pa
that most had ever seen.
He'd beat the cheese out of those tribes
and carry home the cream.

He was raiding in the south
as was his normal way,
when Ripahau arrived back home
intending now to stay.

He had two pages of
the Maori prayer book in his hand,
and the bright idea that he would teach
by writing in the sand.

Katu and Te Whiwhi
had been told to stay behind,
as Katu's dad, the chief, went off
to see what he could find.

He took the fighting men with him
and left behind the rest.
Katu loved adventure too
but this, he knew, was best.

This time he'd mind the women
and the children, that was fine.
Katu had the mana
that could keep them all in line.

Many times he'd fought with Dad
but now it was his turn
to make sure everyone was safe
until the chief returned.

The children playing near the gate
they first saw Ripahau.
Te Whiwhi recognised him
and surprised he wondered, "*Wow!*

*Could Ripahau be still alive?*
*We lost him in a fight!"*
But here he was as large as life—
what an awesome sight.

That night around the fire
there were many stories told.
Children sat in wonder,
as they heard of days of old.

How Ripahau was captured
and how men made him their slave,
and what he got for punishment
if he did not behave.

When he told the story
about learning how to read,
Katu heard those words and
his ears picked up the seed.

"Tell me what you mean by 'read'.
That's something new to me."
Ripahau held one page up
for everyone to see.

"This white thing here is called a page.
It's made of stuff called paper.
The black bits are called writing.
I'll teach about that later.

Writing's made by smaller bits
called letters, they make words.
When words line up, a sentence comes
like my speech you just heard.

You write on paper with a thing
called a pencil in your hand,
but we'll use sticks for pencils
and our page will be the sand."

It was a night of happiness,
of laughing and of song,
and everyone was hushed
when Ripahau went on.

He told them the story
of a twelve year old young girl,
and a chieftain who had killed her
and how that had changed his world.

Next day the classroom was the beach,
the blackboard was the sand,
and he taught them how to write down words
with long sticks in their hand.

It wasn't long 'till they could read
the pages he had brought.
Katu was excited.
It was good what they were taught.

"Don't you have more pages?
Is there more you brought to read?"
"No, but I saw more up north
soon after I got freed."

He mentioned Rotorua
and the 'God Book' that he saw.
"We'll send a message up to them
and ask if they've got more."

## Chapter 21

# The Hide Out

Soon the package did arrive
from Uira's missionary,
and you will be amazed
at what was in it... so let's see.

They opened up the package
and a small black book was found.
It had Ngakuku's name inside
and Katu passed it round.

"This is the book Uira took
from round Tarore's neck!
It's battered, worn, some pages torn,
but, yahoo! What the heck!

The words, we heard, inside this book
have power to change men!"
Katu and Te Whiwhi
couldn't wait to read it then.

Te Raparaha was back again
with war still on his mind.
It seemed he liked the winning,
and he did that most the time.

"What is it my boy does down there
just scratching in the sand
and staring at those strange marks
on those papers in his hand?"

The chief had plans to fight again.
This time he'd take his son.
He sent someone to get him
from the beach down in the sun.

"Katu and Te Whiwhi, bring your friend
and come and fight!"
But they had other things in mind
than fighting day and night.

Katu, he was changing
as the words took hold his heart.
The life of Jesus in the book
began to play its part.

The words in the 'God Book'
were affecting how he thought.
His battles were inside him now,
of quite a different sort.

He sensed there was more power
in love right now than hate
and wanted to read more of it.
In fact he couldn't wait.

"No, Sir!" he said, "I cannot come.
I'm learning how to read."
To this chief though you don't say 'No'.
Man, that's a foolish deed.

"You WHAT?" Te Raparaha exclaimed,
"No one says 'No' to me!
If you don't come and bring your friends
I'll have you killed... all three!"

They'd better go. Can't say 'No'
or they'll be dead next day.
Better think it out again.
Was there another way?

"Of course," said Katu, "I know what!
We'll run away and hide.
I couldn't go kill people now.
That don't feel right inside."

Where could they hide, where could they go,
where they were not well known?
If someone saw them, chances are
the word would get back home.

"You guys, it has to be a place
where no one thinks to look."
Kapiti Island off the coast,
yep! They'd hide there—with the book.

In dead of night without a light
a waka left the beach.
Three men paddled for their lives
'till they were out of reach.

The morning came, one boat was gone
and so were those three men.
The chief was cross, but mourned his loss,
"We won't see them again!"

The chief must fight without his son
and though he didn't show it,
he wondered what had changed his boy
and would he ever know it?

The young men hid and time went by
but no one came to look,
and so they settled on the isle
to read the whole 'God Book'.

They all liked reading it themselves
but there was just one book,
so two would have to wait while one
would have his turn to look.

A bright idea soon made it clear.
These men were onto it!
They simply split the book in three
and gave each one, one bit.

One read one, and one read one
and the other read one too,
then one would share with the other one,
and he would share one too.

The 'God Book' was exciting.
They just couldn't get enough!
But they had to hunt for food or starve
so that took some time up.

There was no shop to buy their kai,
the nearest was Australia.
So they would fish and they would hunt
and seldom had a failure.

They'd catch it, kill it, clean it, skin it
and build a fire round it.
Without one match they'd cook their catch
thanking God they'd found it.

They found that they were thanking God
for more and more each day.
Katu was the first to say
that he would walk God's way.

The one thing that he needed
to free his heart from strife,
was forgiveness from the Saviour
and God's new way of life.

Te Whiwhi was his cousin
and both were very close.
Katu's heart no longer dark,
Te Whiwhi felt it most.

He could tell, and very well
that Katu's heart was free.
He opened up the 'God Book'
and he prayed, "God, please change me."

Now there were two. What would you do
if you're the third one with them
and you didn't want to give your life
to God to be a Christian?

So he stayed cool and as a rule,
although he saw their changes
and liked to see that they were free,
he fought to rearrange his.

Things were happening in his heart
but admit it? Nah! Not him!
Love was fighting hate inside
and he didn't want love to win.

He wouldn't be a 'fern frond'
and give up all his hate.
Bitterness had taken root,
for him it was too late.

How could he forgive the men
who beat him as a slave?
But love was winning in his heart
though hate was acting brave.

Now Ripahau had his own
perception of the world.
That's the way you see things
let me tell you boys and girls....

See, when you are abused
and people hurt you like with him,
you have your freedom outside
but the shackles are within.

Hurting people, they hurt people!
Unless we can forgive
our hurt stays on the inside.
That's a painful way to live.

Ngakuku, he was free inside
and Uira found that out.
See, healed people they bring healing,
that's what **love's** about!

Ripahau one day read this,
"Father, please forgive them."
It was the story of the cross
and something snapped inside him.

The people that had nailed him there,
Jesus was forgiving.
"I need that power," said Ripahau,
"I need that way of living."

He prayed a simple prayer to God
and Jesus changed his heart;
gave him love from heaven above
to make a brand new start.

The shackles broke, the chains fell off,
the slave was finally free.
He had God's power to forgive.
How God does that beats me!

## Chapter 22

# Return to the Mainland

Six months back the three men feared
the wrath of Katu's dad.
The time they spent in hiding
was the best they'd ever had.

But now not one man was afraid,
each knew what he must do.
They must return back home again
to share what they now knew.

A sense of purpose grew that day
like they'd not known before.
Did they meet with Katu's dad?
Nah!  They met an open door.

Welcomed home as long lost sons,
the people gathered 'round.
"Where's my father?" Katu asked,
but he was not around.

Te Raparaha was off again,
fighting with his men.
It could be weeks 'till he got back
so they were safe 'till then.

The people sensed excitement
in the lives of these three men
and wanted to know all about
the adventure that had been....

At first the people noticed
that a warmth was in these men.
Fear had driven them to hide
but they were different then.

A different light was in their eyes,
it seemed they were more caring.
The people wanted them to teach
the skill that they were sharing.

"We'll start by teaching you to read,
then you will understand."
And as they read, the lights came on
from the 'God Book' in their hand.

They learned real fast 'cause they were bright
and wanted to be taught
and once they learned they'd teach their friends.
It's like a fire caught.

No telegraph, no radio,
no mailman to the gate.
No TV yet or airmail jet,
for those we'd have to wait.

No Facebook yet or Internet.
No phone, not even wire,
but north and east and now the west
God's love spread 'round like fire.

Forgiveness was the spark we know.
Tarore's dad, Ngakuku
had trusted God to do His work,
**LOVE** was replacing **UTU.**

## Chapter 23:

# The Power of Love

Then something happened.  Guess what next!
Te Raparaha came along
and as he came back home again
he noticed something wrong.

"What's happened to you folk?" he asked,
"What has gotten in you?
You've stopped your squabbles and your fights.
How come they don't continue?"

"Nothing's happened here at all
except the book we're reading."
The 'God Book' had the words of peace
and on it they were feeding.

"The 'God Book'? Where did that come from?
I can't believe the changes.
Amazing! I must check this out.
This book that rearranges!"

So now the mighty chief himself
had noticed it as well.
The power of Love that changes men
was here and he could tell.

So intrigued was this great man
that now he dared to look.
He said, "I'll no longer be a man of war
but a man of this 'God Book'!"

This was great news for Katu
and the men that he was with.
This meant they'd call for missionaries
to come down here and live.

So Katu and Te Whiwhi
headed north up to Paihia,
to see if they could find someone
who'd come with them back there.

Henry Williams was in charge.
Imagine his surprise
when Katu and Te Whiwhi
looked straight into his eyes and said,

"Te Raparaha is changing
since Tarore's book has come
and we would like a missionary.
Can you spare anyone?"

There was another missionary
and he had just arrived.
He couldn't speak our language yet
but he was gonna try.

They called him Mr Hadfield,
Octavious was his name.
Henry Williams, he agreed,
so Octavious Hadfield came.

Four men left together
'cause Henry came as well.
Octavious was the man for them
as far as he could tell.

They sailed by ship to Poneke (Wellington)
and then they had to hike
up through the hills to Otaki,
without a mountain bike!

Surprises were in store for them
as they walked on back home.
Someone had been calling
and it wasn't on the phone.

In village after village
that they passed along the way,
the people they had learned of God
and knew just how to pray.

Goodness me! How could this be?
Without a mission station?
Well, Ripahau had taught them!
Now it was a celebration.

"What a welcome," Henry thought.
Octavious was delighted.
If that was you, you would be too.
The whole tribe was excited.

After Henry went back home
Octavious sent a plea,
"Five thousand Bibles won't last us
for more than just two weeks!"

The printing press could not keep up.
Good news was all about.
The fire of Truth was raging
And you couldn't put it out!

## Chapter 24

# Forgiveness Bridges The Gap

Ok, we can't just leave it there,
'cause what about the south?
There is this great big island
with some tribes 'down in the mouth.'

Many still were hurt
from what Te Raparaha had done,
so Katu and Te Whiwhi
had a plan—a scary one!

Oh, it was high adventure,
it was very dangerous too
but it had been a dream of theirs
and now it would come true.

South Island tribes missed out 'till now
on hearing the Good News.
Te Raparaha wouldn't leave the pa
for another South Island cruise.

He'd be a man now of 'The Book'
and not go there for war,
so they would never see him there
like they'd seen him there before.

So who was gonna tell them
that they need not be afraid?
And would they all believe it,
that the big chief changed his way?

It felt strange to lay their weapons down
and head to sea unarmed.
For most men that would just be mad,
you'd think they'd be alarmed.

But 'Perfect love casts out fear,'
it says that in the book.
So a compass, and a flax kit
with a 'God Book' is all they took.

They took Tarore's book
which was torn into three parts.
They paddled south for the southern shores
to change South Island's heart.

1843 it was —
this good news must be shared.
This time the mission was for peace
and these men were prepared.

Take a look! This little waka,
on a stormy sea.
Two men armed with just a book,
but wow! Their hearts were free.

They sang their songs as they paddled on
with purpose in each stroke.
I tell you what! Don't know 'bout you
but man, I love these blokes.

Now here's the thing. Your bells would ring
if these two blokes arrived:
Te Raparaha's son and his nephew one.
You'd take off for your lives.

If you were wise you'd realize
their daddy won't be far...
parked up the beach and within reach
to come and raid your pa.

But hang on! What is this?
It appears they have no spear,
no mere and no musket.
Nah! Something's not right here!

"Quick! All you people, take the kids
and hide up in the trees.
Keep a lookout for the rest
and you lot come with me."

No one could imagine
what these men had come to do.
They pulled their waka up the beach
and walked from their canoe.

Something different in their ways
removed the need for fear.
It wasn't long 'till all the tribe
was gathered 'round to hear.

"You know my name is Katu
and Te Raparaha's my dad.
You count me as your enemy,
that really makes me sad.

You see we have no weapons
for in truth we come in peace
to ask for your forgiveness
on behalf of our own chief."

The people looked around in shock,
"Te Raparaha? How come?
That man has filled our land with fear
from morn 'till setting sun."

"It's up to you, but it is true.
He's sorry for his ways
and he will never come again
to hurt you all your days."

"What made the change to rearrange
the heart of such a foe?"
"We have a book and you can look
if you really want to know!"

So there it was. The people longed
to find what changed the men,
so Katu opened the flax kit
and taught them reading then.

Fourteen months these two did that,
from tribe to tribe the same,
asking for forgiveness
in chief Te Raparaha's name.

They spoke of the love of God
and peace through Jesus Christ.
It brought them great respect
for which Jesus paid the price.

Maori all throughout the south
experienced God's power.
**Forgiveness** freely won the day
and prolonged our finest hour.

The bloodshed of our country's past
would one day soon be gone
but the power of forgiveness, friend,
goes on, and on, and on!

## Chapter 25

# The King Maker

Tarapipipi, as we know
built a Christian pa.
The people gave him great respect,
both Maori and Pakeha.

When there was a skirmish
that just couldn't be resolved,
they'd call this great man of 'The Book'
to get the problem solved.

When Tarapipipi was baptised
he sought a Christian name,
so 'Wiremu Tamahana'
is now what his name became.

He gathered friends and whanau 'round
who followed Jesus too,
and from his heart he shared his plan...
the task that he must do.

He told the British Government
his people need one thing,
a godly man to rally 'round.
His people need a king!

A king that would be honoured
by all men in this land;
a king to lead by wisdom's creed,
and he would find this man.

Wiremu prayed and asked the Lord
for the man to fill this space,
what crown to use to crown him,
and for God to give him grace.

Grace is when God's heart is touched
but not by you and me.
It's 'cause His love does not depend
on us at all, you see.

He loves us 'cause he loves us!
Any mother would know that.
She can't help loving junior
even when he's just a brat!

But God's love's bigger than your mum's.
His patience is amazing.
The cross of Christ is proof of that.
His grace just keeps on saving!

The chieftains gathered in the north.
One would be chosen king.
A man that all would rally 'round.
That's not an easy thing.

Many chiefs spoke stories
of why ***they*** should be king.
One man sat right at the back
and didn't say a thing.

But God looks at the hearts of men
'cause that's His kingdom's home.
God alone knew the heart
that would sit on the throne.

Not many days and it 'came clear,
the task to find was done.
The quiet, wise man down the back,
'twas him!  He was the one.

The man who knows right from wrong
with simple common sense
and with it has good judgement,
well, his riches are immense.

Wisdom gives a long, good life,
riches, honour, peace
and pleasure gets to fill that list
King Solomon released.

So it was done, they'd found the one.
Potatau was the man.
The chiefs agreed 'cause they could see
the wisdom of God's plan.

The first king was Potatau
(Not Potato... I know you!)
Potatau was a great man
and the chiefs, they thought so too.

Though there are lands with kings and queens
and stories of their fame,
with crowns of gold and emeralds
and treasures to their name,

our land's the only place on earth,
though many lands are tribal,
that crowns it's regent with a book...
the 'God Book'!  Yep, **the Bible!**

When crowning our first Maori king
on that historic day,
the Bible rested on his head
as Wiremu spoke this way.

"This shows that God rules over all.
He governs both King and people."
God's word alone had changed our hearts—
all other plans were feeble!

## Chapter 26

# The Jewel in the Sea

A kidnapping! Some fish and chips,
and a man called Mr King.
A magistrate with a Maori friend
whose wife could really sing.

A chief who saved some convicts' lives
and won Australia's heart,
and a boat load full of animals
resembling Noah's Ark.

A slave boy prince and a sweet young girl
with a flax kit 'round her neck.
A father's loss and his gift of grace
that time will not forget.

The greatest treasure known to man
in the hands of a slave set free.
Two cousins armed with just a book
to free their enemies.

A mighty chief shocked to the core
at the change of his own tribe's heart.
The story is miraculous
right from the very start.

It's wrong to presuppose that
just because a man is black,
or white, or pink, or green, or red,
that he is this or that!

Men get put in boxes after
they are dead and gone.
Putting them in boxes while they're
still alive is wrong.

If you label someone,
you just labelled you as well.
It's a box you can't get out of.
Soon you both will smell!

Labels keep us separate
but only in our mind.
Think of him then as a friend
and you'll get on just fine!

West Coast sand is black with iron ore,
the East Coast's white!
And you can get steel from the west sand
if you do it right.

The white sand brings the tourists
and they come here in their throngs.
The steel is used to make the ships
to bring the tourists on.

Both sides work together well.
God's clever, don't you think?
Both sands protect our precious jewel
set here in the drink.

Fighting over differences
for years just brought us death.
If we'd continued down that path
there would be no one left!

The great ones in our history
learned how to **forgive**,
bringing love and truth to man—
the finest way to live.

Forgiveness opened up the door
to set our people free.
Let none of us forget the price
it cost for you and me.

Yes, freedom always has its price
and thank God we are free!
Free now to live and love as friends
on this 'Jewel in the Sea'!

**Let's sparkle for the world to see
and let them look real close
to see a family of man,
who love each other Most!**

In the history of the nations
there's an anthem that stands out,
humbly asking God defend
what our land's all about.

Love and truth to all mankind
so we might all live free.
Only God can answer that
so what're the words?

Let's see:

> "God of Nations at Thy feet,
> In the bonds of love we meet,
> Hear our voices, we entreat,
> God defend our free land.
>
> Guard Pacific's triple star
> From the shafts of strife and war,
> Make her praises heard afar,
> God defend New Zealand.
>
> Men of every creed and race,
> Gather here before Thy face,
> Asking Thee to bless this place,
> God defend our free land.
>
> From dissension, envy, hate,
> And corruption guard our state,
> Make our country good and great,
> God defend New Zealand.

Peace, not war, shall be our boast,
But, should foes assail our coast,
Make us then a mighty host,
God defend our free land.

Lord of battles in Thy might,
Put our enemies to flight,
Let our cause be just and right,
God defend New Zealand.

Let our love for Thee increase,
May Thy blessings never cease,
Give us plenty, give us peace,
God defend our free land.

From dishonour and from shame,
Guard our country's spotless name,
Crown her with immortal fame,
God defend New Zealand.

May our mountains ever be,
Freedom's ramparts on the sea,
Make us faithful unto Thee,
God defend our free land.

Guide her in the nations' van,
Preaching love and truth to man,
Working out Thy glorious plan,
God defend New Zealand.

E Ihowā Atua,
O ngā iwi mātou rā
Āta whakarangona;
Me aroha noa
Kia hua ko te pai;
Kia tau tō atawhai;
Manaakitia mai
Aotearoa

Ōna mano tāngata
Kiri whero, kiri mā,
Iwi Māori, Pākehā,
Rūpeke katoa,
Nei ka tono ko ngā hē
Māu e whakaahu kē,
Kia ora mārire
Aotearoa

Tōna mana kia tū!
Tōna kaha kia ū;
Tōna rongo hei pakū
Ki te ao katoa
Aua rawa ngā whawhai
Ngā tutū e tata mai;
Kia tupu nui ai
Aotearoa

Waiho tona takiwā
Ko te ao mārama;
Kia whiti tōna rā
Taiāwhio noa.
Ko te hae me te ngangau
Meinga kia kore kau;
Waiho i te rongo mau
Aotearoa

Tōna pai me toitū
Tika rawa, pono pū;
Tōna noho, tāna tū;
Iwi nō Ihowā.
Kaua mōna whakamā;
Kia hau te ingoa;
Kia tū hei tauira;
Aotearoa

Our anthem is the best on earth.
We started out to put God first
and He protects our coasts from war.
It's in our prayer—that's what it's for.

Yes, freedom always has its price
and may we all be listening...
'cause if we live to love as friends
**this Jewel will keep on glistening!**

# Maori Glossary

**Aotearoa**

The name given by Maori for New Zealand.

**E Pa**

O Daddy!

**Hapu**

Pregnant.

**Kai**

Food.

**Kingi**

(Personal Name) King.

**Kuri**

Dog.

**Mana**

Power, influence, charisma.

**Marae**

A traditional Maori Tribal Meeting Place.

**Ngati-Hauā**

A Maori Tribe in the Waikato area of New Zealand.

## Pa

Fortified Maori Village.

## Pakeha

Fair skinned. (Term given to European Settlers of New Zealand).

## Pukus

Stomach / Tummies.

## Raupo hut

Small dwelling made from native swamp plant Raupo.

## Te Rongopai a Ruka

The Gospel (Good News) of Luke.

## Utu

Revenge.

## Waka

Maori Canoe.

## Whanau

Source of strength, identity, security and support... Family.

## Whare

Maori dwelling.